ACAPELLA RUSH

POETRY IN PEACE

N K JYOTHI

Copyright © N K Jyothi
All Rights Reserved.

This book has been published with all efforts taken to make the material error-free after the consent of the author. However, the author and the publisher do not assume and hereby disclaim any liability to any party for any loss, damage, or disruption caused by errors or omissions, whether such errors or omissions result from negligence, accident, or any other cause.

While every effort has been made to avoid any mistake or omission, this publication is being sold on the condition and understanding that neither the author nor the publishers or printers would be liable in any manner to any person by reason of any mistake or omission in this publication or for any action taken or omitted to be taken or advice rendered or accepted on the basis of this work. For any defect in printing or binding the publishers will be liable only to replace the defective copy by another copy of this work then available.

I dedicate this book to my mother , father and my grandparents .
They are the cradle of my confidence. My brother , sis in law and
niece are the rings that keep me magnetic energised and I value
that very much.

Contents

Foreword

Preface

This is a collection of poems almost all written with a sense of urgency . So the rush. The rush like our Mumbai, the rush of a writer who has a lot to discover and the rush of poetry writing . Acapella as the poetry has been written by taps on the mobile screen , the new age appendage.

These poems were written over a period of a year and half, starting in the lockdown of May 2020 in Mumbai. The poems were all written directly on the notes app on a mobile phone, so they were literally tapped into existence at regular intervals. Many readers found themselves rekindling the joy of poetry reading, writing and sharing.

Acknowledgements

I am deeply grateful to all my family and friends who have encouraged my writing , by being honest, objective and appreciative . Thanks to their push I have gone ahead with publishing a book of my poems.

Prologue

Read to me !
　　　Read to me my first alphabet
Read to me that I won't forget

Read to me of princes and fairies
Read to me of cows and dairies

Read to me as it paces my heart
Read to me as you are my go cart

Read to me from humble books
Read to me of sleuths n crooks

Read to me as I better understand
Read to me so I can withstand

Read to me the charts n galaxy
Read to me a soupy epoxy

Read to me so I know what I write
Read to me so I can right the fight

Read to me of ghosts and ghouls
Read to me of braveheart souls

Read to me so I am not alone
Read to me for we of one bone

Mother Mine

Warm embrace Sunshine grace
Soaken mirth made our hearth
Forever with me Mother mine

Stirring pots sharing thoughts
Folded arms laughter swarms
Sights smells mold mother mine

Shooting straight bouncing gait
Teachers role talking to my soul
Settled deep in me mother mine

Twining flowers henna lovers
No secrets hide emotions tide
Designed my time mother mine

Shortened life ever afterlife
Pouring tribute smiling cute
Blessing as stars mother mine

Warm embrace sunshine grace

Soaken mirth made our hearth

Hug you longer mother mine

1. Musings

Lo To Us!

The lady is back with her camera
She does not want to leave the spot
The peacocks are busy pairing off
The monkeys are bounding
The angles of the rays are lazily warm
I took my own time stretching my sleeping muscles
Slowly rising to unfurl my arms and salute the sun
Lotus poses !
The cement and gravel challenge my skirt
What chance do I have with just a strong spine
Can they give my kind a growing space
I am sure we can grow in clean water terraces
Divinity is all good but we like how we are
You don't have to prove a point by trying to submerge us
Were we meant to thrive for very long in mucky treasures ?
Lotus beauties !

Delights For All

Sweepers delight
Is the autmnal fall

Brooms kiss the carpet
Soft yellow red pink
Farmers delight
Is the seasonal crop
Hands adore the shapes
Round small pear palm <u>sized</u>
Teachers delight
Is the understanding
Faces twinkle with knowledge
Facts meaning puzzles aha
Gods delight
Is in every movement
Folks sense the changes
Music Trees Birds Thoughts

The Journey of A Single Eyelash)
First it was the hair bath
Which unsettled me
I the eyelash
Shampoo face scrub were lathered
I had slid behind the ear lobe
Just at the joint on the top of the ear
Then the hair was wrapped in a thick towel
Much later after the family was fed
The hair was let loose and finger dried
I had made my way to the cheek

The humidity had made the skin sticky
So I was stuck behind the eye glasses
Soon I was not able to see
That happens when things are too close
She could not see either
That her children were growing up
That her work was waning
She was too busy making the motions
I could have been there for years
That's unviable not believable
So two days later
Her daughter saw me
Momma there is an eye lash on your cheek
Make a wish Make a wish
So I was carefully removed from the greasy skin
Then laid over the top of the closed palm
Gentle skin quite unscathed and with a bit of sheen
The palms seemed to have taken the toll
Wish Wish Wish Wish Wish
Wish Wish Wish Wish Wish
She realised something in that instant
She saw it then
Much like a single drop of dew
The journey of the eyelash was fruitful
Was i worthier, part of a band protecting her eye?
And
Coming in to my own what had i given her now?

Did You Raise The Bar?

They said raise the bar
So I did
But then it fell
But I was determined
So I grappled with it
Raised it again
This happened quite a few times
Oye waz happening ?
How do you raise the bar?
You did
Didn't ya ?
Yes
But it comes down again
We told you to raise the bar
You did
I then went out tired
Raising the bar so many times
Can be exhausting
I ran into a couple of children in the park
They were playing catch
Up the ball went from one hand
It came down to another
Then went up again
Came down to the next

O Man! Is there any meaning to this?
The balance sheet looked good
We had a decent profit
The expenditure column
Investment column was full too
As we sow so we reap
But sow you have to
Again! Again! again!
Plot Plough Plant Pitch
Does nothing ever stay up there?
Did anyone ever raise a machan
Someone has to climb one
Now try singing a higher note!

Hail ye Ink Pen!

Hail ye ink pen
Connoisseurs Zen
What a fine nib
The scribes brave rib
Inky ink blue
Flow oh so true
Write kind pressure
Curls toe treasure
Pump pump to fill
Lithe like a gill
Brain heart do heal

Shows how to feel
Text Style alloy
Movement of joy

Calico (The story of peace)
Calico o spiritual calico
Smoky chimneys you grow
Your bright blocks are a story
Soft warp tough weft allegory
Seeds sown in brown soil
Cracked hands pluck toil
Your airy fluffy white
Bursts out a balm to sight
Bullock carts bobbing bales
Truckloads promise arid vales
They synapse at the spin mecca
Electric water jenny charkha
There is a time of resolution
Cotton amidst political persecution
Shuttle and scuttle mix and fix
White black brown antiseptics
The fibre that is so produced
Flax seeded contradiction infused
Giving flight to dreams soothing
Drapes models basic clothing
The world over linen breeze

Cloth lines sarees shirts crease
Block prints natural hues greys
Wonder material bright lays
Humility patience pristine grist
A country was born amidst
Imagined socialist a contradiction
Can life be mere industrialisation
It is left to individuals to dare
To get cottages to generate rare
Designs doilies kurtas patchwork
Khadi woven but losing torque
The globe continues to roll
A skin friendly gorgeous soul
Calico O ravishing Calico
Where did smoking chimneys go?

Let The Good Times Be In Step!
The trustworthy will be leaving
I continue to stare at the spinning top
I twine it round and round letting it twirl
How will life play out
There is no will to write it, not even on sand
What if they disappeared in a puff
Exiting out of the head of the top
In time possibilities shall play

Now they pile up in sprite
Up and up on the whirling top
It's a wonder how they do that
They don't fall, they hop to the next rung
I grab the top and twine shove them in my pocket
<u>*Better a*</u> *bit of thought a lot of living*
May the best times lie ahead
The good times be in step

Tabula Rasa

Tabula rasa was my potter soul
for I held once a steady bankers tell
locked down ambitions froze the dicey roll
as leaves of a shy tonsured autumn fell.
I rushed back to my rooting village tread
tirelessly tracking my argil wheel
peeking from an annual herbal shed
will undulations give an even keel
My hands shook heart raced as I saw a spot
where on would twirl an old ballet dancer
to crimson textured buds inner eyes caught
white flags on wars laden rivers nurture
Twitching in delight slicking my palms muse
brown beaming a graceful vase of beauty
indentations to paint with gorgeous hues
revolving earthy dreams an entity

The Infant Cries Language

The fireworks decorated the night sky
some were busy in queues
sweet queues savoury queues
sparkler queues cracker queues
Round eager eyes watched
the movements perched over
the shoulder, fat thumbs were
sucked to halt expression
Almost all had a wide grin
around ten whites showing
some waited till the correct
exchanges happened
A few were practising rolls
gun rolls clackity clack
boom! the bombs were a bust
was it a time of reckoning?
Was a new truth being sold?
amidst all the new
developments in the new year
the infant was crying language
I heard that, am happy I heard that
I am happy I understood
The infant sounded happy
High above all that

Return their Resource

There was a sudden flash
a feel of loss hit tight
missing a daily sight
a scene of early light
Water bottle in hand
a mother a tot near
some nodding talk and cheer
something to tell teacher
Narrowing eyes few pouts
some alphabets to track
rocking her satchelled back
bobbing eager no slack
When will the bus arrive
neck craned to the distance
eyes sleep no reticence
morning contradictions
Am bereft so I pray
children survive the E course
please can you Lord re source
return their universe

The Toot Of The Midnight Train

The booming toot of the midnightly train

No man no dog no bird no bus no rain
The green leaves are nourishing their light vein
The red rose white lily are smiles again
The child by the tracks does not hear the horn
His little form in sleep curls to adorn
The sleepless are obliviously forlorn
The sound is too far from their nearly morn
The cold of the night and the deep rumble
Join to carry few denizens humble
A city awake on a slight grumble
Is heard by the girl on a word jumble
For her the bogies with a warning groan
Keep company as she is crossword prone
Soon the bass of the gigantic trombone
Rises high above to a cloud unknown

An Acrid Affair

The toaster was not ever as automatic
As I had interpreted pop up as automatic
I put the bread and went about my errands
In sometime I returned to a kitchen of smoke not my errands
I switched off the mains and unplugged the toaster
Nudged open the stubborn windows compared to the toaster
Shut the doors so my family would not awaken in carbonated
air
Then I waited waving and wondering silly in carbonated air

Soon the smoke dissipated but smell of burnt air hung about
So I lit a couple of incense sticks with a prayer as I hung about

Vulnerable Addendum

Hold the shendi and shake em up I said
You could hold by the shika choti thread
Much like Krushna would save us as a last straw
At a spot from where many nerves draw
The outcrop that is left unsevered is the sign of an ego balm
Bow down mister sang boy George hare ram radhe shyam
The international conscious rocks it with the manjeera
There is many a slip between egoism and meera
In this world one does need a bit of momentum
So I say always vulnerable addendum
You never know when I will need a lift
Blessed I am with friends that are a gift
(Glossary of non-English words
Shendi, shika, choti: similar meaning words that denote an
uncut tuft left at the base of a tonsured head
Krushna: Lord Krishna (Hindu deity)
HARE RAM RADHE SHAM: hailing lord rama and lord
Krishna (Indian deities)
Manjeera: small hand cymbals)

The Swing

The swing in the old yard
Called to the passerby
Psst come sit on me
Let's have a joy ride
Now the swing had company
Someone to give it a high
For the children had all grown
To set up swings elsewhere
Swoosh Swoosh Swoosh Swoosh
The face and ears felt the breeze
Reaching the upper branches
The swing saw the man smiling
He had just read about the sage
Who had turned a person to stone
And here was a mere lowly swing
With powers to enliven a mundane walk
The man cleared the overgrowth
Put a board near the swing
It read ' Swing with me for a while
My maker meant for me to bring joy '

The Water Runs

The water does not know what it will do today
It was pumped up last evening
Only to flow down next day
Mind you it does not fall

As it reaches the opened tap
It may be used
To clean rinse but
All it does is run
Then another faucet opens
Someone wants to warm up
So they let the water through hot metal
It has now been heated but continues to run
If the water thought about it all it does is run
Others do things to it
They may freeze it, collect it, pump it, waste it
But all that the water does is run
But the water does not think so much
It keeps moving
If it does not evaporate
It runs

Should I be worried?
The footpath is slowly getting filled
Every next time I see it has more weeds growing
Green sprigs over grey paver blocks with joints
No one to stamp the weeds out
A large tree has been given a border
It does not know the weeds
The border has restricted movement on the footpath
Weeds are rising and they sure don't look up to the tree

No one is using the footpath
The bike stands there
The municipal weeder is not into weeding not every day that is
Coz footpaths have to be stomped treaded
Urbanity has rules of cementing civic society
But what is to be done if the people stopped walking
Where to begin?
Is revolution the only answer

Wait Under The Awning

Pocket of deep depression over the ocean
Is that why the cosmos is weeping copiously
They want to feel one among each other, atmospheres and
humans
The dark cloud and the blues
Quit feeling sorry for yourself
Yes I know you are sometimes beside yourself with hurt
Let it be
The cloud shall pass
Stay in the pocket
You never know what may emerge
A rainbow a poem a therapy
A game a tantrum a jazz tune
You will not wither away
You will learn and grow

As We Wait *! (the nature of inner peace)*
Sometimes it is the wait
that is tricking..
what seems like opportunities lost
what seems like opportunists found
All passing like the stations on a fast train
You can't get down
Are you going too fast
Are you being driven too fast
Your destination the destination
of the train and then a bus and
then a cart and then the drag
to meet the whole
Who is there waiting to hear you
Tell of your life of dreams coz
That had decided to stay and
Mind the garden for you
Your garden the bed of soil
Your garden the sown plants
Your garden your daily habits
Your garden your tiny arts
When you come to your garden
the outside world is left behind
immersed in the soil of structure
balanced with deeds and dreams
You are the queen of the garden

Stretch your toes
Sink into the soft cushion
Stretch your arms look with closed eyes
The sky is white like the pillow
that supports your head
and absorbs the rise and fall
as you heave deep breaths.

Her Quest for Peace!

Her mornings woke with the rays
Cold frozen but warm with hope
Would she find her son today?
Meals cooked house cleaned
She would set out over snow slopes
The years had been routine
The family to raise the sheep to tend
As the unfazed faith that her missing child
Would be returned one day remained
Can't you make peace asked the wise?
Why do you fret and flounder every day?
I am at peace when I look for my lost boy
My heart will find some meaning
As I talk to the powers of the world
They could not protect my offspring
My life feels temporarily whole
As I look trustily for my little fellow

ACAPELLA RUSH

He haunts my dreams my feet walk
Every day is a quest for inner calm

2. Gaia Songs

The Sentinel

I can smell a sweet
nectarine carried
by a light breeze a
sentinel for the senses
The tree stands at
the corner its cycle
of dew fresh scents
close my eyes
I am carried
to a memory of
late evenings cool and
promises of books
The tree is rooted to
the spot as the
fragrance lets me
breathe lungfulls
I am smiling as
i feel light a
oneness with my
happy thoughts

How Do You Do It?

Every stroke a master stroke
Every light a pure delight
Every colour a different hue
Every moment a variable
Every shade heartily made
Can you teach how to do it?
How to be fresh every time ?
Not just a refresh button
But breathing anew all the while
Do you let go completely
Or do you retain some
Tell me how you weave magic
In a instant pink to passion purple
From pure white to vibgyor circle

The Leaf

The love of a leaf
Speaks to me
Stay connected
Sway gentle free

Transform life
Nuzzle Whisper
Tangle in the air
Share prosper

Bask in warmth
Gleeful in light
Let tears slide
Small is bright

Bend not break
Cheer the flower
Soften the sticks
Adorn for ever

Define a memory
Charm artists
The life of a leaf
So many trysts

Sugarcane fields

Sugarcane fields stalks of strength
midget dominions dimming horizons
closing horizons
Torque on the thighs
hunched backsides

as though antennae tales of greed dehydrating
Grey tar laden tracks
pebble stones corrugated
non vicious spinal taps turns roller coaster maps
: Will we find the way :

O The Ma Ma Magenta!

Earthy rooted green
Ma ma magenta
Nimble winding preen
Ma ma magenta
Grassy cushy clean
Ma ma magenta
Yellow centred keen
Ma ma magenta
Tender soft sheen
Ma ma magenta
Cute shapely queen
Ma ma magenta

Panoramic Pearl

Waking majestic merry maker
Muses gently a twirl

Raising cotton cuspy clouds
Confers heartily a whirl
Peeking blue baby brooklet
Bestows quietly a furl
Spreading green grassy grandeur
Graces casually a curl
Laying earth easy expanse
Entices impishly a searl
Arching taupe trusty trekker
Sigh(t)s panoramic a pearl

Cloud Play

I want to scale your generous white expanse
While lolling by those splattering greys
That luring hint of a playful inside
Are tempting as the aesthetic frays
Why do you lay out big white dollops ?
Then also layer small slaty strays?
You know that the largeness beckons to embrace
As the youthful cinereals grapple for praise

Green Auburn Spell

Carpet of green

Cooling when seen

Bottles of dark
Watching the park

Auburn shingles gracing
Fringes lovely lacing

6.45 the Sunrise
Vista your prize

Deep iconic swell
Green Auburn Spell

Twilight Chants

Golden shimmering glass panes
Pretty green leaflets play piano
The light gently wraps herself
A little flutter of orange clouds
Twilight envelops the mood

Lampshades start their sashays
Crickets count the time aloud
Earthen carpets cool the mat
Sounds soften the tall dark knights

Night charms her way again

Will they stay as they are
A sand clock flowing slow
I could exhale my lassitude
Rosewater views on my eye
Inhale gulps of fresh smiles

Evening Conversations

The evening beach was dark
White curls of the sea designed
A wonderful conversation

Spoke gently caressing cool
Asked of the sands to loosen
Come meet the ocean beds

Why do we get to go so deep
While you skirt ever so gingerly
The waves came up a little less

Tempted the coarse shy bits
A few went along for a swim
We will come back with tales

Just look up the starless light
Soon the black canvas will fill
Twinkle narratives by the moon

Over Hill

Oh for a hammock on a dry topping hill
The rains at a distance blowing a roaring chill
A mug full of spiking hot liquid n some grill
A mind empty till the core of the body overfill
Looking long over a green hazy valley sill
Hand folded into the back of the neck so still
Staring deep at a thoughtless abyss so swill
Sound sleep vision combine to complete the thrill

Reflected Story

Gentle waves lap at the beach
Their whispers to all beseech

Quietly excited watch in huddles
Quite happy as moonlight cuddles

Sands silken silvery soft inviting
Picnic play parlay psst anything

Borrowed power so endearing
Unfettered flowing all knowing

Beam on us O satellite moon
Show us to borrow relate cocoon

Lean on each other share designs
Trade jokes do time woes whines

Live in reflected glory do the job
Adopt invite imbibe impel absorb

We will get there over
borrowed moonlights
I merely reflect some
borrowed insights

Red Royale

O you lovely red
Who's house is your bed?

O you pretty pleat
Whom have we to tweet ?

O you intense hue
Can we get some too?

O you lively rose
Whence a lovely pose ?

O you friend of thorn
How do you royally adorn?

Nature's Greet

Blue palm green calm
White strokes glow evokes
Wavy edge silken hedge
Nectar centre insect tempter
Tender plumage lovely homage
Gaze hypnotic effect dramatic
Parting sweet nature's greet

Guru Cadamba

Sharing young sprawl
Sharing supple strength
Sharing fresh foliage
Cadamba Cadamba

Living sweet scents
Living to make zillions
Living to give shade
Cadamba Cadamba

Teaching globular fun
Teaching buddha insight
Teaching stylish settings
Cadamba Cadamba

Cheery Buddy

White n sunny cheer
Pretty bright clear
Mustard inner charm
Wilding wet warm
Robust friendly soft
Grow spread aloft
Climb soak ask
Nudge show bask
Quiet quite will
Allay Nuzzle chill
Fresh shower bloom
Buddy nom de plume

Imagine In Colour

How can you ever... describe such multi
attitudinal colours
Violet of unimaginable
shades a whisper a graze a softness a deep dark hem on the edges
dew drops letting through to the gentle hue
And then some orange nestling peeking from within not saying
much
just there...
They do not clash they stay as they are no moves to blend
Leave it to the imagination of some nature lover who will
gush and sigh
And not rest till
the feeling is inked in black and white to be
imagined In colour

Rain Keeps A Date

Is it 6 or 7 I can't see
It is dark but feels light
It is cool you slept through the dawn
The first scent of the wet earth

A distant memory
A gentle rhythm tapping on the window
Looking outside the roads are drenched
The puddle is being fed
The sun will have a late breakfast
Possibly being mothered by the laden clouds
A smile spreads
You charmer you know the ways of the world
Perhaps you taught us the game of hide and seek
The Sun is slowly starting to peek

Nature's Trail

Walking for
Open hearts of friendship
Open miles of solitude
Open blues Open sights

Walking to
Soaken songs of timelines
Soaken sheen of dewdrops
Soaken smiles Soaken ties

Walking on
Cleaven stones of lifetimes
Cleaven mounts of gaels

Cleaven vales Cleaven clouds

Walking so
Searching Gill of treelines
Searching eyes of beauty
Searching Peace Searching Sense

Rainy Eves

Let me hue you as you go
Carry this canvas at the turn
Your whites wait these days
A promise of crystal candescene

Let me light you as you go
Keep the twin brights at the turn
Your blacks wait these days
A promise of rumbling resonance

Let me clue you as you go
Carve new designs at the turn
Your greys wait these days
A promise of silver semblance

Let me kindle you as you go
Caress the warmth at the turn

N K JYOTHI

Your rains wait these days
A promise of dunking dalliance

3. City P(silent)Lights

The Cobbler

There was a smiling old cobbler
Sometimes was a bit wobbler
He could mend most anything
As his measure was exacting

Torn slipper in hand did we wend
Sure his tool twine would amend
Sandal sneaker pump bling boot
Sometimes hopping on one foot

As personhood a curious sight
His demeanour strangely light
As his fingers worked a while
Third wry third healer third smile

A bowl of water was his magic
As he chose a tool strategic
Blade or thread rust or rough
Wetting with water was enough

Some haggled with him a rupee
Maybe he once fixed a toupee
Most paid him his fees correct
Few fed him a meal in respect

The cobbler a bankable feature
Never left us for want of suture
A bootless run and return fine
If reminded timely of dead line

His work was his main identity
His space held thrifty sanctity
Not many knew his real name
Called him ramu all the same

Street Brawl

Brakes screeching
Yells overreaching

Doors slam
Drivers ram

Animal postures
Threatening gestures

ACAPELLA RUSH

Scruffs grabbed
Faces slapped

Crowds drawing
Fighters declawing

Almost hitting
Senseless pitting

Egoes ruffled
Reason stifled

Internally dawning
Public spawning

Energy sapping
Insurance swapping

Calm returns
Public adjourns

Human gait
Honour plait

A Road For Posterity

How will the archaeologist know where
shall I inscribe how much
my road has particulate matters of
flashes of patches of life

Who will remember the milestone to
St. Thomas the messengers on
horseback on the last avenues of
the vestiges of a greater city transforming
from deep earth to stone and
tar with facetious trees clinging to
earth leftover and cement for company of
birds who return to memories
of once a forest

Shall I etch the trees or dig deep to
draw figurines street acrobats cockerel
costumed cricket matches underarm
bowling dandia through the night street
brawls with swag impatient children
waiting for buses and waiting mothers
walkers of all gaits
and intents retreat from main to
arterial from busy to key

The sounds where will they go cavemen
did not record sounds they passed
through human ears mouth hands bodies how
shall we record road sonics for
the forms change everyday spools to
LPs to cassettes to floppies to cds and
pen drives to clouds to
pods continuing till we
convince other sounding spirits

Kulfi sellers in the early night calling
claiming the magic of imagined
sweet coolness vendors calling out
mangoes seasonally the vessel swappers luring
the house wive's to a chatty exchange ambulance
wails chants of Rama Rama car honks
though avoidable the dog barks and the rat
cheeps and the crow caws we need
not worry, they will survive.

A ha Maybe I shall convince
them to carry the voices of
the road through their mutation of
friends calling out to each other

in code language of gravel tar regular
road digging unity calls of workers pulling
cables sounds of crackers polluting voices
again avoidable but the pitter patter
will always stay to be heard

How will the archaeologist know where shall
I inscribe how much my
road has articulate matters of
flashes of patches of life!

Mithi River ~~~~~~~~~

Lakes >>>>>>>>>>>fed
Over ^^^^^^^^^^^^bed

Salsette's very own
Oily Litter strewn

Clogged chemical dirty vein
Doesnt breathe strain drain

River ~~~~~~~~sith
*MITHI myth***********

ACAPELLA RUSH

Paid. .. price
rise
City

Allies grope
Trickles hope

Revive her
Mumbai S. t. . i. r

(((((Wonder)))))) fill
))))))Debris(((((distill

Give <<<<<<<<<<<<<<<<<back
Let's un pack

RUNNING free
Blue decree

Mithi Speak

I did not flow I meant a river
Phlegm full breath snuffed sliver
Sawdust debris furniture part
Meek orphaned shards heart

Grey dump lathe cotton mills
A mini Nile dirt airless gills
Animal waste... oil paste
You. nothing.to.us waste

Fed by lakes but left to gutter
Overflowed once slimy splutter
Acidic fairy stinky bleary bile
Herculean migraine saved isle

Being fed by Tansa Powai too
We are there we will fill you
Go rise fight for your strife
Alas unlike Dodo conned for life

Telling us I want to live.. meditate
Accept all literacy basic educate
Everything is there I too will
A quiet reality holding until

Tank @ Time

Tank @6 PM
Evening starts and the old people gather by the tank
How is your knee?

Shall we pray together from tomorrow
You heard what the daughter in law said ?
I have a special oil for the back
That 15 no. was taken to hospital
We don't get good mangoes any more !
The girl cannot cook!
Tank@7PM
Evening falls as the children gather by the tank
Hi how was the day
Got a lot of homework
Is he telling a ghost story
Let's play dumb charades
Nice dress where from?
Let's sit around and play passing the parcel
Practise the play
Land and water Land and water
Tank @ 8 PM
Evening deepens the ladies gather by the tank
What did you cook?
Did the maid come?
You heard what the mother in law said ?
Tell me where you got the discount ?
Nala is getting married
That 5 no. has lost his job
Tomorrow let's call the mango seller
Tank Now!
Evening comes but no one gathers by the tank

Red Double Decker

O stocky graceful creature
Balancing the turn on two feet
O crimson gorgeous giant
Loading the tide in two bellies
O slow and steady wobbler
Showing sights one two many
O rounded gentle guzzler
Raining views on prime two seats
O trustworthy old behemoth
Holding hopefuls in two lines
O tringing and honking conveyer
Dropping faithfuls going two ways
O hot bulky steamy bestie
Bidding adieu to sad two eyes
O memorable rouge trendsetter
Resting empty on your two decks

River Ulhas Meets Arabian Sea

A shot of the blue sky the white
clouds the green texture the river Ulhas meets Arabian

sea viewed from a height

I have seen this meeting point cycling
through closely in my childhood reminisces a
friend now from far

The river runs to the sea cheered by
protective mangroves stretching its accepting
arms nothing held back

The clouds join in vanilla clusters for
its the pre rains they paint a pretty picture all
together never crowding

Nature knows the ways of an illusionist The water
the land the forest the sky viewed at a distance they
blend to serenade the parched heart

Sometimes sights fill us as
much as the
waters of the world

Apocatulips

In that smoggy city
With a speck of green

Ran reckless rats
Pollinated pesky pigeons
Crows cawing company
Scared sparrows spying
Bats bawling banshees

In that city on a gutter
With little large hearts
Parrots patrolled peep holes
Mynas maw mawed morsels
Cats crawled car sides
Dogs dotted densely
Buffaloes bounced breakless

In that city with religious hues
A loudspeaker blared a story
Fauna Farm Fairytale
Rains ran regardless
Animal activity activated
Herbage heightened happily
Clung climbed cement
Overran ornate over bridges

In that city with no space
A seizure by greens grew
Burst brizzly beanstalk
Tyres tangled tree lines

Engines evergreen energy
Wheels winged wondrously
Yellows yaying year round

In that city now holly changed
A metamorphosis mushroomed
Ruling reigned rabbit holes
Violets Verdi voluminous
Quelled Quite Queenly
Swayed Sashayed Springers
Arrived Amazing Apocatulips

Mumbai Local

I love my local train
Can't find a safety chain
How am I likely to fall
Am sandwiched as a ball

I take my local train
What a view at 7AM rain
Like riding a water shower
Long ago they switched power

I get my local train
The city's iconic vein

Overdoes it's populous load
Bless you if you are able to board

I share my local train
Toots friends hobbyists gain
A petty bargainer's delight
Quick the vendor will alight

I love my local train
Plies in floods never vain
Ubiqutous elastic iron house
The key to Mumbai's viscose

Golden Circus

Circus wide eyed golden wonder
Celebrated rings knives thunder
Footsteps air borne hand stand
Somersaults tightrope live band

Juggle trapeze hooped towed
Round world eighty days road
Covers centre folds applause
Ringmaster clown fire fullhouse

Virtual blindfold lifts shroud

Madagascar reminded us proud
Tents tops tricks tramps treats
Unicyclists riders retro feats

Astounding children old alike
Entertainment marvels dirt bike
Online shows giga mega bytes
Celebrate new age stunts sights

Lets walk across golden sands,
Creating footfalls memories,
Follow us across the lands,
Let's celebrate new trajectories ...

Raining Yay Yay!
Raining..yay yay yay
Pours torrents in September
You awaken chilly at 4AM
It's raining rain.. Yay Yay Yay

Should I sleep as I absorb it
Or should I match roar pour
It's pelting rain.. yay yay yay

Sleep lulls warm bedcovers
supine rises falls rhythm n rain

It's dream rainzzzz..yay yay yay

A cooling clang wakes you at 8
Banter of rain metal pipes ping
It's rain hard n fast ...yay yay yay

No presence or feel of that sun
Cooling dark with whites above
It's raining steadily yay yay yay

Maybe cherapunji london
Bhopal Matheran or Kerala
Raining worldwide yay yay yay

A ripple & A fish

We had great times being together
Right by the tornados the gales
Our powers gulf many oceans the weather

I remember how we swam easily into the sea
I a ripple and you the fish from a school nearby
I soon joined the gigantic water whirlpool tree

You continued to coast the warm city sea
Only to be chased by inanimate floaters

How has your journey been my friend are you free

That one time when we flushed up the rocks
You wanted me to show you the life of the urbane
We quickly slid back to our rustic sandy flocks

I have since joined tsunamis and storms albeit natural
I read somewhere that your beach is too grotesque
Remember when the child wanted to blow a fish bubble

Memories are hazy but I do see the zone
We had a great time you and I children of the sliver
Of nascent hope like our friend the skimming stone

Acapella Lush

Today the choir was a zillion long shush

The sky opened her lungs thunderous arush

As the earthy cappella unleashed in bass

Steely translucent notes descended amass

The timbre was a silver wet running hiss

N K JYOTHI

United cries pelting chants not a note amiss

The earth gushed clouds burst frogs jumped

Her children awoke hearts thump thumped

4. In A Lighter Vein

Farmer Zindabad Laddoo Zindabad

Did you enjoy a plate of wheat and rice
Did you sense the ghee melt in a trice
Farmer zindabad laddoo zindabad

Can you feel the proteins nourish your day
Can you feel the glob in a gleeful sashay
Farmer zindabad laddoo zindabad

The greens and reds neurotransmit cells
The missable crunch spreads to roof jells
Farmer zindabad laddoo zindabad

Hands sow reap cut thresh for us
Orbs hold mold you sweet bulbous
Farmer zindabad laddoo zindabad

I want our farmers to feel safe n sound

I want the laddoo to continue as round
Farmer zindabad laddoo zindabad

One feeds souls stomach life and content
One gives spirits joy belly and merriment
Farmer zindabad laddoo zindabad

Rhyme Of Mistaken Identity

Do you want iron out a case of mistaken identity
Walk among the by lanes of our inner city
Covered up shams spew holy dust in grey realty
Epics were out shouted all in contralaterality
Look for the red balding bumps in the locality
There is nothing left to argue in your duality
Go deep right and no sitting on walls of banality
What app FB twitting wasted tabloid ditch creativity
We can speak the language of notionality
And so did the workers of this stocking community
Lead by engineers mastered in civility
Started at street level looking for a ethnicity
When they saw the open mouthed red gullibility
Depicted the fire hydrant as a monsterity
They decided to seal off all watering anitpathy
Lathered blobs of cement in sentimentality

Hopes of submerging pipping political dynasty
The hydra had to be mistreated with some ferocity
Put it six feet under to stop its fecundity
What better than to fill valves with morbidity

My Kewl Friends

They come to meet me
Slight drapes of chill
Sneaking friends of mine
I welcome them thrilled

Playfully they graze up slow
Seeps quiet bumps an arm
Spreading a little cool
I wiggle toes lightly charmed

Ankles receive elfin glances
Fun times in climes over rule
Gaming is silently afoot
I tiptoe fizzy warming pooled

Mild freeze flits unsuspecting
Wanders about sock or lock
Pondering if shawl or shiver

I see cosy memories stocked

Their cold does waver in a day
Hearty grins the sun shadow
Whispering to the elements
I pray linger nip sleep endowed

Round And Round

Do the cycles of life go
round round and
sometimes square a
half to be found?

Do you seek to meet in
leaps and in bound a
singular static I
captured as you frowned?

Does the meeting happen so
seldom you surround your
self in layers layers of
selves sights so sound?

Did you see there it

is your core all wound in
colourful turbans new
roots growing over ground?

Doth enjoy Shakespeare as he
did famously propound all
world is a stage of life and
you the actor renowned?

Doff clap for yourself as you
cheer laugh clown weep a
smile hug dance as fresh
selves do expound?

Solecism

S olecism is a ungrateful
O mission without knowing though
L icenced to poets allowing them
E ccentric eclecticisms such as the
C ats whiskers become whats caskers so garbled
I diomatic idiosyncrasies which Freud called
S lippages of the tongue that may cause
M indless mayhem syntactically in etiquette

(O)

I blur on the circumference of the o
Last evening I remembered pi
As the water washed over me
Something about equality
Another construct it seems
Does the water know pi
Does pi no about water

I come back to the o
Flashes of an oval garden
No not for real
Just the words
OVAL GARDEN
Not pi
Something about inequality
That's a construct too
Flashes of oval garden
Like in the cinema
Did cinema teach us how to think
Or did cinema reflect our
flashy thinking

Got back to the o
O it is like in LORE
Not 0 as in AC 2020

The Gestalt context
Equality inequality context
Chuckles inside me
Maybe I can use it in class
Or maybe I won't remember

Transience is permanence
If you can get
A hold
(O)

The Smart Aleck

Once there was a thoughtful lick
That wanted to be smart and slick
The lick rolled on the poetic tongue
To be lyrical in an adventure sung

First the lick seared as a hot pin
A goth tattooed her dimpled chin
Then to lick the echoing steam
Got to be the cold of an ice cream

Next the lick by the dog did find
A stick playfully tossed behind
And of course a lick in passing

As the cat smirked by sassing

Quick lick of milk by a mother
A phoooo phoooo on the lather
A header a lick of blood dirt fear
As a goalie kicked the ball to clear

Toward the close the smart aleck asked
A metaphysical what to be unmasked
In my next cycle after a flick like this
Will I be that sniff smile or a trench kiss

The Sun Brushes The Sky

The sun brushed the sky
She had no time to dye
So he asked the racing rays
Could you reduce the glaze
Not in a mood for mellow
Let me play with the yellow
Streaked shades of light red
Drew orange tracks of a sled
And when the sights did please
The earth folks smiled a crease

Half Moon Coffee

Had to wake
a voice spake
of deep feeling
lay not ailing
sympathy cold
discomfort unfold
curl cool feet
hands in sheet
but the middle
half warm half hour
of sleep left over
squirrels chick crow
heard no sparrow
woes in slang
no yin yang
thick fresh cream
sweet with steam

Magnetium Aka Attractions All

Wee Tring call
Booth Ben toll

Cam bodhi Zen
Blue Pottery yen
Simple Iron magnet
Flower lady signet
Wise Yin- yang meet
Indian tri-colour greet

Idiomatic Webinars

A Bottomless Sit
As it hits the nail on the dead(points)

Apple of the Sigh
As also darling of the passes

Touch (Screen) potato
As one goes ananas

Footprints on sands of whine
Out of sight and out of mindlessness

Ignorance is effortless
A hard net to crack

Kills many turds with a stone

Die a dozen coz it's rule of the numb!

Cementing

It's all around me
That dry grey feeling
It can get my throat
Like a sub sahara
Some phlegm clearing cacophony

It can settle on my art
Redouble the art
Draw some cement dust designs
Not very valued
But may appeal to best from waste

It guzzles the rain absorbs selfish
The arid dry nose drying effect
Parched skin you could draw figures
Dry skin sketches
Maybe put it on You Tube

My rainy days have no fragrance
Neither of earth nor of coolness
A uniform tyre tripping ripping

Eye burning steadiness
Don't envy the tar laden pot holes

Lowdown.. Isms..

Stitches in time or roll on the floor promptly
Better late than never coz early birds may drop the worm
Procrastinated the thief of time coz
he went early to bed but was late to rise
Time and tide wait for no man thankfully women
may not mind this
Idle mind is the PJ workshop
Unnecessary is the key of reinvention
So make masks as and when the sun shines
Hahahahahaha is the best pill
as I double up during the Lockdown...

Trip Tease

A clear road
Ride at ease

ACAPELLA RUSH

A gentle curve
Sift a breeze
A deep gorge
Stun to seize
A verdant flash
Wave o trees
A gigantic rock
Sink to knees

A lofty climb
Sure we try
A cloudy float
Wisp oh my
A dollop drop
Grin and sigh
A water fall
Cool coo cry
A mighty bird
Take me high

A lightning bolt
Flash and cease
A thunder boom
Jolt and freeze
A beating heart

What a tease!
A ruffled bed
Soft and crease
Back under cover
Snug and peace

Fruit thrillers

When the watermelon hits the floor
have you felt the
loss
At
so
many
levels

When the lime is squeezed
into a water glass ...
how it
t
o
r
p
e

d

o

e

s

to meet the honey..

Unrind the orange and ..
Feel every
p o r e
of
your core
rising to meet grasp ....that ...zing

The plums of our times..
Sink teeth through smooth skin..
seeping ..
bitter tangy sweet ...
can you ever
com part mental ise ..

And the mango...
always ready to tango
and cash
on the greed to reach

through fleshy
fibres of ecstasy

Scrabble

Scrabble is da game
Called many a name

Lexulous Scrabulous
Lierati fabulous

Tiles max of seven
Likes rax to haven

Ticktock ticktocks
Wordstock wordrocks

Set across cross-legged
Play down now webbed

Beware anagrammers
Pestiferous scammers

Winning is the aim
Fit words lay claim

Players wranglers
Excited anglers

Long new rare mix
Two one seven six

Aa ab ae ad
Qi li po ed

Triple double word score
Twice thrice letter s'more

Dictionaries galore
Beneficiaries encore

Would It Be A Stretch?

Stretch yourself as you wake
Elongate?
Watch a dog stretch in the sun?
Arch?
Stretch fingers to fan out stress
Widen?
Stretch wet soles on warm mats

Drain?
Stretch your luck for second helps
Try?
Stretch the time with kith n kin
Spend?
Stretch the truth to save a friend
Lie?
Stretch your spine in cat pose
Yoga?
Stretch the mind to entertain
Imagine?
Say stretch n watch your face
Almost a stretch !

Stationary Bike

I am a stationary bike
Sometimes with a psyche

I was thoroughly cycled once
To burn calories of buttery buns

I could see cable a TV serial
As she flexed knees bipedal

Then my duties diversified
The corporate slid did snide

I was made to hold books
The attempt to improve my looks

I did not know the way of Jeeves
Repartee through laden sleeves

Recently I was posted on OLXa
A few offers but no Alec or Alexa

Who Done It?

The painting is not original
Curator says clutching in horror

Where is the original ?
Owner lisps via smoke rings

The authorities did not swap it
Manager avers rubbing brows

Nobody has stolen it

Detective nods twirling handlebar

The video cameras don't lie
Security pips shoulders drooping

The scanner showed this original
Technician covers up fists

We check it everyday
Expert waves log in hand

Tomorrow we call all
the thief shall be revealed

So who done it
Chief wags his finger in doubt

Sleep As You Like !

Some sleep when they lay
Some sleep as they flay

One slept like a fish
Another slept with a dish

Some sleep light as a feather
Some sleep on new pleather

He slept like a log
She slept as if in a fog

Some talk in sleep
Others walk in sleep

I sleep some more
You sleep and snore

Some sleep not
A few sleep oer a shot

They study sleep circle
Their sleep was a miracle

Some sleep bored
Yet others sleep ignored

Last they slept to dream
Now we sleep a requiem

Rhymeozones Cacophones

Caw caw caw caw caw caw
Care to feed me O maw
Brr...whoosh ..Honk honk
Going through a new bronc
Craaaaaaw .....Craaaaaaw
Humankind .....pshaaw
Cre craw cre craw cre craw
Fly by shut eye with draw
Whooooosh whoooooosh
Breaklessly no shushshush
Trrrrr trr trrrrrrr mehe mehe
Hope this does not stop midway
Music Noise Bikes BirdOphones
Surround Glean No RhymeOzones

My First Internet Friend

My first bonding internet friend
As we both fell in witty trend
Was on Mukha Pusthakam
Technical doubts overcome

We laughed at the Indian twist
Facebook had a sanskrit tryst
We tested poke security post
Virtual buddies making the most

As we poked we felt the pain
O dear how much we all feign
Security of post seemed a stretch
So we checked for random letch

Logged out in hope n disbelief
Of imagined glitches causing grief
Intimacy given an E branch
Unaware of the friends avalanche

Evil Elopes With Humour

Hush, don't be loud,
Hush, the evil may shroud,
Hush, cower shutter,
Hush, calm your flutter...

Oops sorry about the squeak
Oops there almost a shriek

N K JYOTHI

Oops blanket don't slip free
Oops nearly sneezing spree

Dang when can i openly talk
Dang the media covers that walk
Dang how long this lying low
Dang where is the up risers flow

Aah at last a tolling of hope
Aah she cut the hands' grope
Aah the earth is cooling down
Aah my mates found renown

Bah all this clamouring clang
Bah humbug coz I have my gang
Bah of course they sow on slopes
Bah the evil with humour elopes

The Fun Train

Tickety tack, trackety trick,
The train rattles our back a crick
We bounce with its rhythm,
Swaying bouncing in momentum

Pitter patter putter potter
The train slurs as it splishes splosher
We giggle and goose bump
Rubbing our out held hands la forest gump

Glinty glint wonky wink
The train warms on iron snugly slink
We stretch and sneak all aglow
Catching sight a timely awesome rainbow

Grunty Grunt screechy screech
The train pulls up the hill a jolly reach
We get up and dust our selves
Hopefully catch sight of jaunty elves

Strange Climes

I thought it
was Summer
simmer brighter
scorcher

The Evenings
lit till late
great strait

consummate

Heated my
Bones relaxed
untaxed syntaxed
minimaxed

Supple detoxed
warm Body
sweaty gritty
already

We laid Beans
to dehydrate
dessicate crate
not irrigate

which

Tauktae in its
wake precipitated
soaked cloaked
choked

Dramatic change

in Weather
blather nether
slather

New Climes
fused mush
puppyhush
lush wood thrush

Stellar Way

Girth however has come to stay
We lade lade and lade away
We got to show mirth a stellar way
Laugh laugh and laugh every day
Look brethren the worth of gray
Not let dollops of statistics mess our say
Wonder work art in dearth are they
Gather our imaginations let us pray

Thai Chilli

Thai chilli crop is growing
What to do

what to do
They are falling to the earth
Pick em up
pick em up
I put them in a white bowl
Wash my hand
wash my hand
They sheen and they preen
Click a snap
click a snap
Share the picture with buds
Pals I mean
pals I mean
A garland on my doorway
Elves at play?
elves at play ?
Dry roast the pungent spice
De seed them
de seed them
I can powder them n macerate
Zingy condiment
zingy condiment

Poppy Tune

I am a disco dancer

Elvis like romancer
I can boogie woogie
Zap you with a noogie
Vow you with shades
Of poppy red in glades
Keep your feet moving
Friends together grooving
Feel an unequivocal high
Smile for the end is nigh

A Tree House

A tree house is for joy
A gigantic natural toy
More than a tall machan
Quiet a dream caravan
Strong open rooted space
An alter ego birthplace
Innocent as a childhood
Swings of tarzan robinhood
Nightly exciting starry chat
Minimalistic creative habitat

Blossom

Firm strokes
Gentle gradients
Breathing easy
A beautiful sight....t
Poise prose
Equitable poetry
All ingredients
To triumph.....
Random spirals
Shakeups
Mutations
Alien invasions
Incomprehensions

A Road Less Marvelled !

We found the bark of a tree in our way
Fallen brown thick broad coarse drying burlay

Our car would not make the jump ride over
Would our time be lost or the forgoer

We wept stomped raged but dusk did overtake
Before we left and made it through the lake

We did not reach on foot in anyway

A deer looked us in the eye far away

Amused in animation like the chimps
Grazed on fresh happy leaves with just a glimpse

Squirrels symphonically bridled of sorts
A new species here all hisses thumps shorts

It was raining and we had locked us out
The snakes could not see the panic about

Did they rise to the test to scare the scared
What more could they do when they were outstared

Out came the forest tribe and made our path
They took the wood we the road to a bath

A route which had more tales than intended
Embellished milestones suspended

A road less marvelled had this up the sleeve
A tale to recount full of joie de vivre

Why Birds of a feather clock together?

Birds of a feather clock together

Punch in punch invisible tether
It's not their plumes but whines gripes
That lend perfectly like pugilist swipes
It's the path that times their life
Coz endings starts need a fife
The camaraderie of sharing woes
The energy to bounce to break the inertia
Their daily travels stations destinations
Their motivations conversations frustrations
Make for good airing dusting venting
As the hours of work chores goals play out
These avian souls then seek their ally
Make a quick getaway to re-enter other realms
Temporary bye bye till we meet again

Ginger Pome

Ginger rhizome is like the submarine
Can sting to heal though looking quite serene

Low red yellow grows around four feet tall
Defensive potent pods of gingerol

From zingeberacaeae family

Makes ales antioxidants easily

At home in tropical spring time climes
Turmerics cardamoms drawn to limes

Upset tum poem of singebera
Flintstone gingeber Hana Barbera

Hope animation jumps off the flapper
Brings down the bloated perks up the lapper

Gingerly the cat ran to the village
Literally an unsteady image

Unlike cuts of this spicy condiment
Easing steadily many an ailment

Go Sail /)
Tall graceful the sail
Lassoes the rushing flail
She holds the wind by hand
As it pushes at her band
Woven tales keep engrossed
Lest the direction be tossed

N K JYOTHI

A nimble mother deer
Herding direction steer
Almost a trampolene
No bounce just vaseline
The gust that tries a sleight
Monkeying is set straight
Funny smile for a comic
On point timely ergonomic

5. Anecdotes

Battle Of Waterloo

Napolean met his waterloo
Sadly badly so did my broom
Willy nilly to battle a cockroach
Chinese meal meek screacher

Snatched from the nail
It was swung into action
Smack whack on the cockroach
Sneaky crawly flying creature

Ducking brandishing the broom
The tap was hit and the water ran
Swish Mish at the cockroach
Brown black antennae feature

Repeated hits to the ground
Walls whacked ropes fraying
Shoo phoo at the cockroach

Pronotum belly winged teacher

Hitting out to an unseen end
Splitting the broom sticks
Boo hoo at the cockroach
Disappear crawl broom seizure

Frog Spider Squirrel

Waiting at my bus stop
I see a man at a distance
He seems to have a smile!
Little unkempt, walking to me?
I continue looking at him

Turning to a lamp post
I see he whips out a baton a rope
Fixes it arm height on the post!
Is he an acrobat with a paint pail?
I am giving him all my attention

Leaping frog spider squirrel
I see him landing up the baton
Harnesses waist to the post !
Will he wave with his free hands?
I am brimming with anticipation

Perching on the first baton step
I see he whips out a baton a rope
Frog spider squirrel fastens perch!
Frog spider squirrel fasten perch?
I exhale as he is close to the top

Perching on the top step
I see a paint brush in his hand
Paints from top, down to perch!
Did he hop a baton rung down?
I look to applaud but not a soul

Continuing with my fascination
I see he freed the top most baton
Paints down to perch!
Reverse frog squirrel spider unfasten paint ?
I note a frog squirrel spider land unfasten paint

What just happened under one minute
I see now he has disappeared
Adrenaline filled nothing to do!
Whom shall I tell this to?
I bob at the bus stop waiting

Clarified Butter

Looking at the pantry
I check a few items
Oil Semolina Salt
A packet of ghee

Looking at the prices
I put them in the cart
Two packs one Kilo
One pack and one litre

Looking at the pay options
I enter the details
Wednesday two at noon
Gift packing available

Looking over the balcony
I nod to the security
Orange Covered Down the gate
Your packet is awaiting

Looking at the time I think
I go as soon as I can
Vessels washed breakfast done
Vegetables cut all ready

ACAPELLA RUSH

Looking at my eyes I wink
I get down the steps
Crow black packet orange
Concentrated poking

Looking at the crow I shoo
I rush to the spot
Little rends a few holes
Neighbour tsks Packet picked

Looking at life I think
I could have gone earlier
Quarnatine the packet
Look for problems later

Looking at the packet I see
I note the leakage
Smells like ghee feels like ghee
The crow could it sniff

Looking at my hand I know
I heat the molten ghee
Others cleaned and shelved
Poem I got to write

I look at the page
I open the dictionary

English Ghee Translate
Clarified Butter !

Anecdotes

When pictures come alive
Fond merriment does arrive
Actions imported from life
Relive rejoice reminisce rife
The narrator listener bind
Harness relation in rewind
Lessons are learnt remote
That time capsule anecdote

Like masterful Mark Twain
They amaze reamaze rain
Tilting gradually their head
Scratching ears they tread
Shifting stances tone gait
Taking one across state
Emotions replay in ampule
Anecdote that time capsule

They rejoice you rejoice
Recreate image by voice
That moment this learnt

This moment that relearnt
Imitating roleplaying the tale
Watch youth eagerness regale
Remind recount redraw rime
Anecdote that capsule time

Lighthouse

You thought a lighthouse was to navigate....
But I climbed a lighthouse!

Steps steps steps steps steps steps steps steps
many more you can imagine coz I was climbing
then
hunch not bend or stoop
step out... stretch
back straight
watch your head
imagine the armada at a distance and you are
royalty welcoming them back from a little shopping trip
coz Amazon would not deliver your favourite sweet then.

No lights in the light house in the daylight on one land
it's partner in the other is working
a beacon steadfast to ward off or wave its
presence though they are missing many cousins

twice thrive removed for techno sensors did them
a disservice the giant was left with no shiva
eyes just melted glass solidified fitted ready to shine
electric or otherwise no smoking zones

We held hands as though a testimony to our
common dreams broad horizons aerial dances endless
blue green teal ripples foam tides ant like ships boats
vessels recovering the lungs for we would soon
turn our back in the behemoth
hunch
step down
you got the picture
descend the steps
steps steps steps steps
steps steps steps steps.

You thought a lighthouse was to navigate....
But we climbed a lighthouse !

A Forest Bloomed
When the canvas tugged she lifted
her pen drew a curve
and her students streamed in

she differentiated with them
canvas forgotten
A few days on the sheet ruffled
the canvas called back
so she he added some strokes
sketched green leaves whilst
fleshy mangoes were had well in time for calculus
Many months passed before the canvas
rolled out the birds were missing and so
were the boughs flowers inked
them on paper as her heart booked
lips smiled her brood looked on proud
Finally it rained heavens opened stars
fought for the view as she put the final
touches a flick here there nibs scrambling
flying colours rhythmic etches breathing life
:lo and behold the forest bloomed:

6. I Ask

Why Mellow?

Why mellow as we grow in age
They say wine gets better as the years go by
Go to sleep on a laughing page

Open your mouth four letters rage
Ouch I bite my cheek to reign the words that fly
Why mellow as we grow in age

Crying tears weep woes umbrage
Time to try tricks of the hand roving at sly
Go to sleep on a laughing page

Dress younger party books pillage
Come swing your hips move your feet not to shy
Why mellow as we grow in age

Do your weeds don't mind spillage
You lurch you will you arch you try
Go to sleep on a laughing page

Who will help you at older stage
Nyeh! don't let such finalities in mind ply
Why mellow as we grow in age
Go to sleep on a laughing page

'A New Born ?'
The night started young
Can the night be a newborn ?
The seeds of the dawn
The egg of the morn
The placenta of the personhood
The womb of the day
Gestatation with the sun
Developed in minds
Delivered by the evening
Pushed pink glory as twilight
Yes Now I Know
Not just the night ..
Everytime can be
not just ....
Refreshed !Restored ! Reborn !
but ....
'A NEW BORN '

N K JYOTHI

What is Priceless ?

A stolen morsel greater than a jewel,
In the middle of the day
As the tiny hands grabbed
The bread from the plate at the pawnshop
A mobile lay on the dashboard
They could have sold it for money
Desperate snatch for cloth is all

A stolen conversation from a busy parent
The smile on the child's face
The satisfaction of being heard
The gift was left on the sofa untouched

Is Life A Lesson?
As a new born learning to crawl
As a youngster spreading sprawl
Life tosses cues are at every stage
The soul essences used to gauge

Some have learnt life's lesson
A few used a Smith n Wesson
One may have given up on life
Another slept with others wife

Many have lived in a template
Others made others contemplate
The heroine had a famous story
The villain given the tale of gory

None will know the tests' extent
Except the one who felt militant
What others see as fight of might
Many may call it right to fright

One day the final call shall come
Another realm none overcome
Nothing to carry but a dusty self
A charred end or embalmed shelf

The blazing light may blind an eye
The searing pain will nay you die
The lessons will continue to guide
The spirit of life will help you tide

Who Goes There ?

I live cheeping in the forest road
Atop the tall peaceful canopy
My days always freshly load
Filters of blue red orangery

I am in the bed of the ocean
A treasure trove to be unshackled
Eons have passed in emotion
Find me so that a life is brightened

I reside in the valves of her heart
Beating folding swelling with her
Every time she bests a chart
I run amock gleeful dancing tiger

I am the thought running in mind
As every test he passes true
Glory every sculpture of his find
Unseen places heraldic queue

Why Does The Mother Cry?

The days were unending as were the nights,
She waited and waited and waited,
But there seemed no hope in sight…

Where had humanity lost its flight
Would mankind ever be sated
The days were unending as were the nights

She could not bear her children's plight

No she couldn't let them infected
But there seemed no hope in sight

They wondered whether it was her might
That had released a strain unwarranted
The days were unending as were the nights

Humans were seen as though struck by fright
Locked in their homes bolted
But there seemed no hope in sight

All they do is crave heights rights fights
And they think it's her that's fated
The days were unending as were the nights,
But there seemed no hope in sight..

How The Earth Resolves?
She rotates and she revolves
And wobbles on her resolves
Her journey drops at sunset point
Refreshingly dewed a dawn anoint

We can cry and we can well up
Ends are beginnings as chin up
When she is rayed upon anew
Our sleepless bleary eyes renew

Dream wish plan and wait
In the pauses keep it straight
See how see accepts her past
Healing is as strong as a mast

Who Is .Freud?

Freud the great psychoan<u>a</u>lyst
May have been a physiologist
Was by no means a sexologist
Sigmund you keen hypnologist
Starting of as a psychiatrist
W<u>as</u> sadly never an oncologist
Freud the popular psychologist
Dabbled early as a neurobiologist
Maybe called a free associationist
Schade! A mere projectionist ?

Can I Live Like This?

Pluck thoughts that perk you
Blood of your heart the simmer
A dish to exceed tasty smiles
Cycle colourful grand tracks
Etch fine grateful meaning
Blood of your heart the thresh

Unknown dreams farming peak

Ski down white sheets of snow
Mind body curve new angles
Blood of your heart the pen
Calligraphic tales of bravery

Zoom past bustling bazaars
Pluck delightful wares unaware
Blood of your heart the coins
Materialistic realism greedy joy

Ride tunnels largesse bellies
Swimming slow cool surprises
Blood of your heart the train
Rattle rouses giggly flashes

How To Fill The Oil Jar?

Why
Do you
Want to live
All your life time
In moment squeezed
Heart beats will out last now
Work will take own its sweet time

The spill will be more than you know
The rush fill cram jam lade jar so box
Numb teeth clenched hands grab tight no wood pecker
Notice jiggle move your neck feet breathe out
Loosen the limbs arch the back
Roll the tongue look around
Angle the pouch gently
Eye look hand hold
Moments go
Jar Fills
Oil

Did Maestros Feel Write Music So?

Tree
Leaves sway
To music
Unseen unheard
Don't try to sense
Just waltz along the breeze
Rhythm of touch and not a sound
Did maestros feel write music so
Swing in the arms of a curving bough
Galactical cadences a milkyway

'Was this a 'Not a year'?

Naught a match by any standards topsy topsy topsy no
turvy flattening everything but curves it's
November and we can call it a
'not a year' only fear

Staring everyone in matchstick held up eye totally
Tom bam clang bidaang roadrunner has finally
been laid to test 2020 is the booming
exploding latest

News channels are back to basics like counting numbers and
getting wild children to behave on debates and
chatting celebs so that man woman like 2020
is confused

What else is there to do besides mask sanitise cook clean eat
poop care forward backward pause ventilate
webinaries online online online online
virtually a standstill

Countries are running albeit politics people are running away
albeit
restrictions lives are running auto some are ticking till
the winding will give way
head stuck in sand for many reasons

Nobody tries to make sense except the yearling nobody
is truly silent except the higher
power watching <u>2020</u> mowing earth
like an Armageddon

What Is A Walk?

Heel sole foot toe
Heel sole foot toe
The first few steps are in gratitude
To the mother who will always, bear you
Stride swing stretch flex
Stride swing stretch flex
These are to meet in solitude
With oneself who is always, there for you
Pace face smile grace
Pace face smile grace
Could be to tell the grey n greens
I have come as always, a visitor to your world
Nod race greet breathe
Nod race greet breathe
An exchange with self and others
Hail as always that all is well with you and I
Further stronger faster weaker
Further stronger faster weaker
A cyclic rhythm of maintenance
For a rightful place as always upright on the earth

Cooler lighter slower calmer
Cooler lighter slower calmer
The final wave of recapture
Getting back to your soul as always,
for the body has been exorcised

Who is Viktor Frankl?
Viktor Frankl the logotherapist
Suffered Dachau as an attitudist
Chose to Listen with interest
Saved by love for dearest
Wrote Man's Search for meaning
Now common ultimate in healing

Can You See It Go!

Take a breath in
See a breath go
Watch a scene around
See some thoughts go
Make a morning bread
See the softness go
Clean and sweep and mop
See the gratitude go
Sit a moment to ponder

See the minutes go
Prevail through your day
See the evening go
Lay at night to sleep
See some spindles go
A few drops is all it takes
To see the ocean go
Take a deep breath in
See a heavy breath go

What Is The Fa In Father?

Fathers are mothers with Fa
Funtastic Firm Fastidious fancy
Fathers are brothers with fa
Finer fairer freer founder
Fathers gather but with fa
Frenzy finance ferocious fetching
Fathers are like weathers with fa
Fiery freezing falling fleeting
Fathers are feathers with the fa
Familial favourite frank forming
Fathers lather you but with fa
Frothy farmer fermenting ferrule
Fathers are fathers with fa
Firm Facilitative Further forward

How To Do The Loop?

Loop the Loop
Loop the song
Loop the day
Life is in loop mode
Loops are not as loopy as they look
A deft left
A languid right
An overthought west
An unseen up
Live the loop
You know not what
A Little hiccup
Regurgitates! Shakes up! Rips apart !
A unsung tune
A hidden abyss
A burnt vessel
A kernel of fruit
At the end of a point
Look back
Stand tall
You are the hero
You designed
A beautiful loop
That has you spellbound

Break free
And
Start again!!

Can A Man Will?

The sun can rise
The moon can set
The rice will cook
The cake will bake
The sea can wave
The wind can howl
The car will run
The bus will ply
The tree can stand
The root can hold
The ski will ride
The cart will pull
The land can bear
The fall can stun
The pot will stew
The tea will brew
The time can wait
The hill can heap
The axe will fall
The mill will work
Gaia Can !

But
Man will !

Why Is Time My Favourite Element?

Time is my favourite element
Time will come time will heal
All in good time
Time is full on fun
Time pass time share
There is always time to play
Time travel can hurt
Not to 1805 and never 1941
Those were among bad times
Time is metaphysical
Time as sense time as soul
It's time to question our mind
Time has no patience
Here now gone in the next
Now is the time of fret
Time is a treasured memory
Time with Ma college time
Here feel the valued time
Time can be neglectful
Nettle needle wheedle
Then time to turn a blind eye

Time is a revered seer
Time as focus time to transcend
Just a time to meditate
Time is all encompassing
Time is eternal time is everlasting
What a wonderful tome is time
Time is my favourite element
Time will come Time will heal
All in good time

How Did The Bear Feel Well-Adjusted?

Imagine a big bear
Paws that are bigger than its body
Carries iself and goes around anywhere
Can shrink only the paw

So stops and shrinks
Goes about it's normal routine
Eats kills plucks thwacks prunes
Doesnt expand paw unless needs to move

Wonders why only paw can shrink
Rues that other parts can't
Frets tries stretching exercises
Should I see a magician a psychiatrist or scientist

Then Covid hits
Bear realises at least I can move on my own without walking
I can compete with humans who can walk but now can't walk

I can carry myself
Yay yay yippe yippe I am ok with my paw for now
Anyway scientists magicians psychiatrists are physically distanced
from me

Can You Do A Witticism?

Put on lightly a jest a joke
Gags up wile a slight a poke ?

Caper to be some funny
Scamper and dive la bunny?

Make a face so others laugh
Did it look like their gaffe ?

Come let us learn to humour
Find a strength of the consumer

Lament on the shortage
Of their potential wattage

Time it right , say the unsaid
The ideal let's a smile spread

Wisecracks may not work with all
Some have hearts that could loll

Kidding with said pleasentary,
how does man witticise his donkey?

You can run a pageantry
but can I swing nee monkey??

Who Is Dr. Skinner?

Instrumental was Dr. Skinner
Teaching human bread winner

Condition either by reward
Or Punish with untoward

Take away something precious
Take away another abnoxious

Random or consistent wait
Fixed or variable rate

Elementary like dear Watson
External acts no ingestion?

Scientific clear prolific confident
Skinner's pigeon mice competent

What Are Keys?

Keys keys musical keys
Play me a beautiful verse

Keys keys archival keys
Find me a bountiful lore

Keys keys amiable keys
Match me a soulful yang

Keys keys lockable keys
Open me a cheerful room

Keys keys sparkable keys
Drive me a zestful jeep

Keys keys unreachable keys

Feel me a grateful hand

Keys keys misplaceable keys
Make me a mindful one

What Are Keys?
Jingle jangle jingle
Bunch of steel keys
Sa re ga do re me
Musical melody keys
Hmm there hmm where
Buried within in tote keys
Kitch kitch hitch hitch
Stuck in lock jam keys
Tick cross tick cross tick
Marking system answer keys
Thump thump thump thump
Matching loony heart keys
Oh shoot I am a fruit
Where did I put the keys
Make many many copies
One each neighbour keys
Scratch fit turn Asd423
Unsolvable coding keys
Heee haw heee haw hee
Cool life hack key

Where Are The Good Spirits?

There was this spirit
A friendly one it was
Maybe getting offended
I will clarify how to address____

So _____ ghost loved to roam
Saw all the things __ wanted
Zipped from place to place
Watched dear ones at life

It had rained considerably
The roads were flooded
People on the street were less
Maybe a blessing _____ said aloud

No one could hear no one saw
_____ continued to go around
Spirited soulful smoky starling
Watched over a quieter city

As day ended ____ myth reported
Slid sneaked one day at a time
Happy to see fleshy bodies

Make the best of tough times

Many such metaphysical beings
Haunt the trains buses schools
They chatter laugh and smile
They are happy about their temporariness

Do You Feel The Rhythm?

Busy cutting on a chopping board
Kids playing on a snaking board
Others trading on a virtual board
Did you start a rhythm?
Listen to the knife go tak tak tak
Listen to the dice go drr trr drr
Listen to the gui go clik clik clik
Do you hear a rhythm?
See the veggies go flop round flop
Hear the squeals go sha neh weh
Sense the mind go how wha whoa
Did you find the rhythm?
Feel the makings of a yummy boo
Real takings snaky ladders true
Deal shaking busy emarts too
Do you feel the rhythm?

Do You Feel A Surreal Counterbalance?

Who knew it would come this
We do nothing but things happen

Sit at home stay safe lockdown
Work happens money is made

Numbers rise statistics scream
Doing a great job flowers strewn

Life's crossroads both fraught
Welcome new normal be a bot

Innards stew roast lines redrawn
Fight petty scores citizen con

A cloak of fear a stroke of mope
Covert compassion reigning hope

History geography economy art
Science research teaching apart

Life is so surreal real everyday
Counterbalance see saw all the way

What is a Class Act?

A class of eager minds
With books and pens
Sitting restlessly for you to begin
Coz they have a zillion to do
Catch up meet up plan up
They will give you that much
You can do your dance
You can try a trance
The energy will be with you
The synergy will be around
Go do your writing erasing
Go do your talking asking
They will ask back
They will tell you some
They will play along
As the sand clock flip flops
Their eagerness does too
As the bell rings they will collect
Their collective energies
Pour out bounding and all ready
To take on another discourse

Are These The Semantics Of Life?

Notes of linear growth,
A stated ordered story
A little digress is of worth
Research a layered history

Great books written in prison
Great epics were about exile
Great fiction about love arisen
Great shows do extras profile

A history always in retrospect
A story unfolds in bits of writing
A history has a rear view aspect
A story can change with editing

Digress or move as is needed
Growth in life is one name
Digress to grow unimpeded
Growth is digress varied game

What Else Do You Feel Besides The Rain?

Can you Feel the rain moisten your air
Hear the roof banter upstair
Sniff wet earth no cemented lair

Don't let thoughts in you blare

Heart beats to rhythm a dare
Walk a path lest fear ensnare
Save no images even if spare
Don't mull of goals to prepare

Hear the poets as they share
Idyllic times are found so rare
Sun moon stars earthy welfare
Don't lose time to stand n stare

Live NOW as you deeply care
No sense of time to compare
Let life add plumes to your flair
Don't dream of riches solitaire

Is This A Good Enough Formula?

Look into your hearts
Some flowers bloom
They are red orange purple violet

Look into your blood
Some chemicals run
They are sodium potassium chlorine

Look into your soul
Some spirits drawn
They are of peace strife life

Look at your clothes
Some threads run
They are cotton poplin wool

Look at your plate
Some dishes laid
They are veg grains meat fish

Look at your behaviour
Some actions there
They greet meet cheer kill

Where are the differences
Don't tell me it's all the same
How can you n I be one name

We have our likeness but that's it
Celebrate the diversity if so
Evolution always supports it's own

Don't make false claims
Don't worry about your choices

N K JYOTHI

You are just a manifestation

Live your life do your best
Stay alive at any cost
Live and let live

But if you could do a kindness
Be generous polite accepting strong
Evolution also has to change

7. Avian And Other Tales

To The Crow

A blacksmith drummer
No bass just ferocious...tapper
hits at the window pane

The wicked grey tailed gent
Socialist as they brood...decent
craw out passing of brethren

The black hole of a habitat
Swallower of sticky snot...that
cleans for trashy ill litter ates

The cloth hanger thief
Sneaky cricketing cheeky...brief
scores a sloppy pile of sticks

Avian dark dicey zinger
Freaky tease flying over....clinger
smacks the lazy head

The Shiva who can
Stare death by the beak...span
Takes avataars in flight

A janitor an ancestor a dot
A smart aleck pet........ mascot
Demon but in tales sought

D for D_____?

You talk into the night
Do you narrate your day?
Hmm! So like a woman
You curl under the car
Do you miss a roof?
Hmm! Weak need protection
You walk with the girls
Do you run with the boys?
Hmm! Play is for children
You lap the milk
Do you miss your mom?
Hmm! Thats not for grownups
You waste on your back
Do you want a scratch?
Hmm! I am untouchable

You pad around the block
Do you walk your tail?
Hmm! Karma will get back
You quietly made your home
Do you want to stay?
Hmm! Am already there!
You maybe man's good friend
Do you have a name?

Orca Whale

Whaley whale
Orca's tale
Matey mate
Delightful state
Weighty weight
Royal sleight
Gilly gill
Being chill
Gamey Game
Gamboling fame
Dancey dance
Oglers chance
Beauty beaut

Humans loot
Freely free
Scots decree

Sparrow

Brown white streak
Fluffy slight chique
Quick fleet essence
Chirp quiet presence

Flutter fly near
Expand frill fear
Sneak shy peek
Tap tiny beak

Nip spread grain
Eat weed slain
Look sharp hawk
Gaze gentle gawk

Drink calm water
Perch little totter
Hole nest stay
Fragile funny play

Bats Visit

First day of heraldic national geographic
Screeching swooping batsy traffic

The cemented environs transform clueless
Crows parrots vamoose soundless

Swinging second gentleman's robes reminiscent
Tiny hand over hand march merry blind ascent

Brown sweet innocent energetic batlings
Harken cuteness charmers la Ryan Gosling

A mischievous cat climbs for attention
Firefighters alarm two am rescue mission

Fruit laden tree wiped clean by fourth
Chagrin of car owners cleaners behemoth

Leave loot fruit picnic splotchy mess
Quite lane crows parrots back in business

Triddle Truddle Trigdle

The squirrel called out early
Triddle Triddle Triddle
This is squirrel

I had marked the tree clearly
Truddle Truddle Triddle
Am I barking a wrong spiral

Someone do not react merely
Trigdle Trigdle Triddle
My sounds are neutral

The ants have moved generally
Trigdle Triddle Truddle
They are quite central

The squirrel went on demurely
Truddle tridssle Tridsle
I am nutty sometimes feral

The squirrel ?? is quiet surely

——————— ——————— ———————

The mind and body are level

A Bird Dream

Let me tell you the story
of a bird who stood all solitary
as it slept in the night it dreamt of millions
of shards of love reaching the world
springing from the earth sharp but loving
warriors proteins if you say each soul
receives it like the lilt of a those invisible
prayers being sent across the realms and
when the gentle waves of the stream rippled
the bird changed legs and willed
itself to dream some more

The Eagle

The eagle
Splayed
Wanted to get in touch
Thought it had lost
A spine
A measure of the awesomeness
Yen to feel
Discover the skies
From dew kissed carpets
A far cry from its lofty aerie

Why Did The Coo Coo Come Late To The Party

It met the gossips
They had heard the tree was no more
Big blobs of tears
Overcome with grief the coo coo
flew around
Asked cousins
Looked for the crows Nest
One lane had it all
Bat Parakeet Crow Myna Sparrow Pigeon
But my tree my tree
It stayed there among ...

A commotion was loud
The sky filled with birds
Dropping laden whispers
Coo coo could hold no more
Flew into the zone
Spruced trees red flowers
White flowers yellow flowers
Fledgling papaya plant
The
Coo coo coo coo coo
had arrived

Late but ready to party

Reprieve In The Rain

Sorry sweet sparrow sorry you got hurt,
We did not know you were at grain stuffing,
We did not know it would rain flooding dirt,
It was sunny when we heard you fluffing.

Are you warm can you rest now, does it pain ,
Don't lift your head or open eyes dear one ,
The rain is your heart beat on the refrain ,
The cushion is for your rest till your done.

I feel better now that you are healing,
Asleep your feathers tremble to keep pace,
Like the quiver of a bosom feeling,
My bed is blessed to be your soul space.

There you are all ready to take free flight,
You petite beau of my vicinity,
In retrospect the mixed appearing sight,
Shall now stay a nestled happy entity.

N K JYOTHI

One For The Myna

If you are captive
Not by your free will
How would you cope

A soft billed brown bard
Called common Myna
Yellow socked social

In captivity
Apes the handler
Nice friend you arreeeee

When in the free wild
No monkey owl snake
No to mimicry

As the inmates
Ape out the holder
Get up ! walk straight! Heeellllll

Captured souls do dare
Captured souls do dare
Captured souls do dareee

8. Vulnerable Addendum

A Final Frontier!

Something about a shot put
It was not the grace
Neither the strong torso
What amazed me was the neck
Of all the darnedest anatomical structures
It was the neck

The neck doesn't take the weight
It doesn't push the metal ball
It doesn't hold the dead weight
It is a temporary resting spot
The ball does not rest on it

Just help me hold this for a while , will ya ?
It may get scraped or pushed while doing so
Apply some chalk on it that should do !

A joint
The final joint if you know what I mean to say

We Carved A Table Today

We chipped at ...
soft arguments
A particular stubborn idea was lathed over
We are very social in the way we etch a motif
Only that which catches the fancy
Or that which challenges the masthead
We had a moment when someone laughed uncontrollably
It caught on resulting in random knicks cuts
Giving the table some identifying marks
Only the makers would know where to look for it though
Overall the work was regular chiselling scraping crafting
Repeated tapping standing and watching from various points
Tomorrow who knows if the table will be there or get
Taken by an astute patron

With oneself

Sometimes best is solitude,
To separate from the crowd,
So none about will intrude,
As you mumble tales alone

You pace around or sit too
As ideas poems flow
When the sun goes peek a boo

Your hero feels tad mellow

Your thought train in a tunnel
Dark unpleasant memories
The whistling pot turns channel
Brings you back stirring at ease

I me myself spryly change
Like leaves red brown green yellow
Rise and descend walk a range
Like notes on a tall cello

Great Poetry

When you read great poets
you wonder how it never ceases to amaze that
there can be such creations with so
little and so much meaning as though
small is meaningful and meaningful and
seamless and newer meanings unfold as it
hits you square in between your brows till you
have to shake your head and
adjust your posture for it takes more than
the mind to imagine together the multiple spaces the
poetry traverses all with economy of
package and gallops of mind and heart and fill your
lungs again because these poems

breathe as they leave you breathless till you
exhale and pause and walk about a
bit so that another stroke can settle in to
the density slathered with
layers and layers of assumption and
I can go on

Breathe And Bow

As the day opens I ask of thee
Am I you or am I entirely free
Then why have you made me small
Your watery blue sky so infinitely tall
Why am I a soundless white speck
Your candyfloss grace blesses in a fleck
You made my irises in a few colours seen
You kept the rainbow and all in between
Now I ask one thing of your eternal OM
Give us closure for the ones with no home
As the harmony of the five are early to sow
Breathe breathe breathe breathe breathe n bow

I Caught Time

I caught time
Amplified its sound
The whispers

Were not mine

The core was talking
Hot lava hisses
The poodles met
Planned to flee

Godly bells on earth
Chimed in mars
The unheard pleas
As she was broken

The turquoise eel
Sliding in the ocean
A conch re killed
In chariot tales

The first clasp
Mother and child
You can catch your time
Maybe sniff it or some

Eternal Battles

Happy are the countrymen
Greet the valiant
Halos are bright and full

A saint was always in prayer

Little oil vats jubilant wicks
Dumplings fruits sweets
Bathe clean cry heal
Make merry talk love

The sun will rise
Illuminate it shall
Ten was a number
Shall we pit sow build .....

Eternal Spring
A stone house comes alive
Spring is always round a corner
Burst of colours deep shades
Vines and Browns entwine

Then in the soul of hardship
Blood phlegm pus gore
A childhood finally wins
Run textures finally a rainbow

Sacraments robes incenses twirl

Rising raising hopes multiply
Spirits stars galaxies holes
Millions of promises steadfast

Mother Mine
Warm embrace Sunshine grace
Soaken mirth made our hearth
Forever with me Mother mine

Stirring pots sharing thoughts
Folded arms laughter swarms
Sights smells mold mother mine

Shooting straight bouncing gait
Teachers role talking to my soul
Settled deep in me mother mine

Twining flowers henna lovers
No secrets hide emotions tide
Designed my time mother mine

Shortened life ever afterlife
Pouring tribute smiling cute
Blessing as stars mother mine

Warm embrace Sunshine grace

Soaken mirth made our hearth
Hug you longer mother mine

Mirror Gilled

A silver mirror in my
dusty room,
showcases all in an encompassing ray
Does it lift everything with it's glinting bloom,
or was it hit by the golden sunray...

I entered the prism to Narnia one day,
for I wanted to meet Aslan and maybe Dumbledore
Were sliver bronze and preciousness in
interplay,
or did my imagination run away once more ...

The reflection of my dreams in a lake,
are breathtaking and adrenaline filled
Halos all over like my cheval they make,
or at odes of freedom fish like gilled ....

Seven Plus Or Minus 2

I don't have any conviction
Only doubtful searching fiction

Seven plus or minus two!
You can add one
So what if the Sun rose today
It may not set having missed the elevator on the 40th floor
What if the coo oo bird cooed at 5PM yesterday
I did not hear it the day after as my snooze extended beyond her
call
So the next door octogenarian said something funny to me
Now I wonder if the others understood us and need they?
The milk cycle clanged at 4AM on the newly mislaid footpath
I wont be surprised if the local management gives silencers to
cycles
The area vigilantes warned off traffic that was a nuisance
What if they got the street corner kid on skates to reroute Google
maps which the trucks don't use ? Who?
The papaya tree started its climb again slowly
What if the leaves looking over the shoulder twisted to change
the double helix , what would be climbing?
The diwali lights come every year from china I hear
What if we string up anew costly china everyday for five days
and at precisely 9.59PM we snap the string for five days ?
Why should I be assured that the kids will come out firing on all
cylinders at 8PM to play
They may come at 8.01 and go back by 8.02 ...only to come
back at 8.03 PM or not
That's empirical evidence for you..
Seven plus one

Still not so sure though

How I Row My Boat

*The mating calls of the coo bird echoes through the yellow rays of
the sun and the particles are seen making way for the romance .
The hammers against the wall the floor the ceiling thud to tell
me there is denseness and some where there is insensitivity .
The reminding triddles of the squirrels echo as they are busy
scaling trees, balconies, footpaths much to their concentration .
The dreams rise ; a distant apparition of laughing, leg pulling,
'sliding off the seat to land on the butt ' times; in real space coz
the time machines had not been activated, it was just a few
satellites and a few space stations.
And coffee; mugs full, hot, sweet ,aromatic , sloshing as we
moved them to make way for pages of homework; fat volumes
where the print pantomimed in scrawls, slants, illegibles,
rewrites, erases cursive, thick strokes, thin strokes.
Mind you I am absolutely no armchair philosopher just a new
age traveller jumping trucks and plying ferries, boat loads of
ideas thoughts trying to rein the water pony; wanting it to gallop
or trot as I please.
My oars row in wavering waters, amidst the chants of the
soothsayer making his rounds; well wishes filling the cool air
with small cymbals that peal , for what is greater than trying a
different rhythm.*

Nothing Train

Is one always moving in nothingness
I heave into the train in all stiffness
Like a fish I had hooked for amusement
No idea about a mass movement
Do juggernaut pullers exclaim in meme
Flash! faces! blank verses ! aargh! what's the name!
Careful there! you totter you unsettle
Missed the train! do zilch ! hiss like a kettle !
Now a realm of non active transition
Fabricating for speech composition
Remember how the monkey grabbed water
Neither drank it nor did it not scatter

A Ride To Reality

At the curve on the road I miss so many smiles
The sturdy wide bark hides
Toothy grins in peach pod
Flowers are lowered lite
Soon to be out of sight
When the road stretches long
Cheerleaders wave aside
The grand trunks to provide
Yellow springs a red song
From eyes to soul they speak

At woosh they are a streak
Soon the road climbs bridges
There is fresh company
Tall branches canopy
Green visions blue ridges Oh so cool!
We both fly All the way down high-five
Now we ride on the ground
Eagerness looks to find
Arches generous twined
Intense fuchsia so proud
Bench marks to fill quickly
Path to reality

Wait For The Sprinklers
It is intensity that comes to the rescue
A self sustained inertia
Transformed to meaning
On the cusp
My lap top refuses to start on saved power
It needs the strong rush
Tyres on the wheel
They take the brunt
Is the wheel not dizzy at all
Repetitions dear not gradients
Of meanings lost and found
Of reaching to flimsy images incomplete echoes

Wait for the sprinklers to start

Go Figure!

The world said it was her day
so she told everyone that it was her day
and she did feel a tad happier
told herself there was something special
smiled at others a little wider ..
then loose weight on full stomach said the message
go figure !

Save The Seeds Of Love

is there no other way
stop the war I say

did it really have to
come to this status quo

who is protected
who is attacked

if you are for kenosis
dance a metamorphosis

put your palm above
save the seeds of love

now i cry for all those
who are now in loss

what education evolution
rue its resulting fruition

Elevated Emoji

It was me and the perching pariah kite
We stood sans our mundane worldly tethers
The bird had risen elusive elite
I had come up with no fashion feathers
Broad black wings had been loosely collected
As the hunter widely scouted scavenge
That thought had me achingly arrested
Saw urbanity's alarming challenge
I sent some hesistant cheap cheeping sounds
He scanned about for the sourceless source
My little thrill trilled knowing gleeful bounds
Imagined a beautiful God of Norse
Later i heard his dual err err err err
He was playing back my trickety track
Seemed a jolly sort of funny fellar
I could tell by the care of licking lack

He opened his wings swooping synergy
Ready to soar to a top rooting reach
Left me an elevated emoji
Facial figures that long distances breach

9. Pot Pourri (poetry styles)

Clerihews

Tarzan the apeman
Swung before spiderman
He lived in the jungle
With flora fauna did he mingle

Calvin the dear boy
Can never said to be coy
Chats readily with tiger stuffed
Talks imagined but not bluffed

Phantom the ghost who walks
Can hear pygmy drum talks
He saves the day and the lady
Kit walker for adventure ready

Birbal Akbar's court jester
Nth Jewel as a wit tester
Dealt with woes in humour
Laid rest to gossipy rumour

Sherlock the sleuthing Holmes
Booked criminals not gnomes
So elementary dear Watson
Deer Stalker cap not Stetson

DIAMANTE

Anger
. Red Intense
Raging Blinding Seething
Enabler Hotheaded Cool Enabler
Soothing Cooling Spacing
Peace Green
Calm

Theist
Faithful Trusted
Idoling Hymning Candling
Godly Ritual Ritual Non Godly
Existing Singing Kindling
Faithful Trusted
Aethiest

World Soccer
Graceful Fastpaced
Dribbling Toeing Heading
Dance Samba Python Warfare
Running Tackling Knocking
Wholebiodied Mammoth
American Football

To Be
Live Exist
Thriving Striving Jiving
Breathe Celebrate Distance Avoid
Rushing Hoarding Exploiting
Deny Overkill
Not to be

Foodie
Drooler Palette
Slurping Tasting Filling
Greedy Indulgent Denier Portion
Fasting Skimping Spacing

Control Palette
Dieter

LIMMERICKS
Illusion

Illusion no delusion
Seemingly an elusion
Senses framed by needs
Maybe the ego feeds
If near real, eases solution

Tube light

Tube light a thing of past
Did not meet an end so fast
It had a choke
It had a starter
Long confused has LED to last

Painting Squirrel

There was a nutty squirrel
Who was to paint a mural
He curved his self well
His bush tail swivel
Made master pieces plural

LA SENRYU
a leaf pirouettes

loosening gravel Well! they say
a silent prayer

Stars moon stars venus
Bright dependent bright special
All natures children

People cross apace
Adjust thine gait keeping own
who leads the play

Mirage of desert
Gold diamond sun copper sea
Illusions varied

Sky cries orange red
Blue master sides calming greys
That battlefield question

CRAPSEYS

Jeep

Jeep is
Open invite
Speed free windy plast faced
Living life on the run to live

Controlled

Miracle

Life is
Most unexpected
Experience tell tale
Miracles unravel your need
Indeed!

Siesta

Siesta
Body relaxed
Comfortable noon stretch
Eyes closed steal core warming snooze
Revived

Pixie lights

Pixie
Lights seem twinkling
Soundless cricket dangling
Recreate tiny lumes by turbines
Starry

Friends

Friends hood
Good to hang with
Fret you for you with you

Earth Pit
No hangover spirit
Heart wired

(14 lines Sonnet)

The Lone Streak

Rising early in dark I hear the road
It called on me to take a private walk
Four am not a soul maybe nestling N lode
Na! the pull did not listen to my talk

Dressing with butterflies the steps I ran
Deep breaths in the pre dawn calm I look
Only streetlights to see the odd milk van
Right in the centre of the road strides I took

The sense of belonging was so immense
Right left left right arms up down gleeful march
The blood coursing my heart was so intense
Whence dream upon me to fill up thine parch

Etched forever in my heart that lone streak
The path the lamps the steps the rush all speak

ACROSSTIX

Irritation

I mpatient to get it over with

R ankling I get to the stove

R ather make it or never

I mpulsively I decide a recipe

T ense coz I want to prove I can

A ngrily I chop the vegetables

T winging for I have my doubts

I red that I am tired and hungry

O ld one-two an onion tomato

N uisance to cook and eat

10. An After Lesson

One day i sought adventure as i could
only imagine from my easy chair
in my vision i had to ride the train
and thrills would come quietly unaware.

i told no one as i went to my work
place with a satchel packed of basic needs
after hours i would call home to say i
am going to have some escapades

Got my ticket boarded the shuttle filled
with many a weary homebound folk
i stretched myself after the crowd waned as
the chugger stopped on a rusty vale fork .

The loud groaning engine woke my snooze as
i shivered in the early evening breeze
at the cusp of urban to rustic scenes
scrunching my nose at the filth strewn at ease.

Outside the railings of the stop of a

sleepy hamlet hung an ad of a troupe
for men to come wind down with a beer some
sides happy hours though not a hula hoop.

The compulsion to rhyme was not there then
as i awaited the big electric
which would further my quest for i was just
four hours into it not yet quite centric.

And the shuttler did make it on time with
folk returning to their localities,
my heart beat a little faster coz i
would be single no familiarities.

Unknown stations startled me sideways
letting me decide how deeply i went ,
into novelty afore the dark closed
to put me in a guarded settlement.

Happily for me i got a nice stay
and was all curled up drawing the curtain,
passing the night time cautiously with no
mishaps shockers of that i was certain.

Sleeping all alone on a strange bed far
from the nest was a bit monotonous,
jittering at every little sound i

soon set into slumber voluminous.

My getaway had plans to visit a
mountainous spiritual hot spot,
for that was known to me second hand in
anecdotes that my friends talked about.

The dawn crept in booming toots of
ferrous engines grinding to a halt,
as though pushing an inertia so strong
moving their weight on parallel asphalt.

Slipping from my warm bed i got ready
to visit the abode in sahayadris,
firstly a top breakfast to celebrate
my maiden trip solo no shaking knees.

i caught a bus and set off into the
eastern rays to my rendezvous divine,
the ride was uneventful dull rocking
alone with foliage and a ravine.

The shrine was impressive the lord consort
left very much to their own devices,
detached etched in stone as devotees sang
prayers feeling blessed with their premises.

i took my boons in the hot afternoon
the sun staring with long reverse shadows,
i walked downhill escaping buses plying
to continue being on tapping toes.

Taking many turns i unknowingly
ran into a tribe of Adivasis,
with no pucca houses sparse clothing i
gestured for water mildly with unease.

After well water to drink smiling strange
i wondered if I had cut their ration,
and then caught a bus back as I was done
with my walkabout in trepidation.

A sweet boy chatted me up coz he was
aching for the home which he had long left,
To get educated in the city
that lay at the feet of a rising weft.

All along the messages i received
reverberating from mountains to land,
was that ' we are not all alone out there '
unseen energies give a helping hand.

i was late reaching home and had to spend
it outside my door coz keys were displaced ,

with my impromptu trip and return at
the graveyard shift when ghosts are released.

So far yet so close from my comfy bed
i slowly reran my trip in my head,
as i wanted to go and crash but that
end took a while as i calmly waited.

Every part of my journey was mindful
Careful yet free watchful but blissfully,
i had taken a trip with I at the helm
as two days went by so meaningfully.

What happened the next day beat all my life
lessons changed me overnight gave me wings,
my scholarship came unexpectedly
allowing my life to my own learnings.

www.ingramcontent.com/pod-product-compliance
Lightning Source LLC
Chambersburg PA
CBHW031308160726
47993CB00001B/336